A CLOUDLESS
MIND

A exploration into the
true nature of YOU and
those you lead

BY

PAUL SMIT & SCOTT BYRD

CHAPTERS

01

Storytellers

02

The Clouds

03

The Cloudless Mind

Preface

Typically, this is where we would recruit a famous CEO to reassure you that we – Paul and Scott – are exceptional performers in our respective fields. This is where you are comforted about our expertise and fed vague platitudes designed to make you excited about what's to come. This is also the section you always skip because you have better things to do. So does the CEO author, who gets his communications assistant to write these sorts of things anyway. So let's just move on to the introduction, shall we?

Introduction

Here is where we would normally explain to you what an amazing book this is and how everything you will learn will blow your mind and transform you from a struggling manager into Alexander the Great. But you didn't pick this up for hype, you picked it up for insights. We won't waste your time with promotion. We trust that you have a discerning eye and are capable of testing the information we present against your own experience. We aren't here to sell you a quick-fix system or convince you of a progressive management style, office plan, or approach to team-building. We are here to share foundational insights that cut through the noise and change your experience of life and leadership. Let's just get to the first chapter and get moving.

CHAPTER

Storytellers

Now that you made it all the way through the preface and introduction, it's clear how committed you are. It's our hope that with all of the energy saved during the introduction and preface phases, you are awake, fully engaged, and prepared to see an entirely new perspective on the world than the one you've been living with for your entire life. Yes, that's a big statement. And we mean it.

It's been said that 70 percent of all leaders are stressed out and weary from anxiety. Obviously, these aren't the leaders that have read and embraced the insights in this book. The last thing a stressed-out leader is capable of is experiencing effortlessness. Deadline pressures, people issues, and shareholder demands are experienced in a way that gives rise to tension and constant frustration. The enlightened, effortless leader sees the world differently. Through understanding the true nature of their own mind, a relaxed, powerful state of being becomes natural and durable.

To be clear, you won't have to listen to vegetarian

music, and we won't be pointing you to a new mindfulness meditation practice, some cool new breathing technique, or even the latest leadership models. We'll be working with hard science to deliver radical insights. Grasping some of the concepts in this book may be a struggle at first. But don't worry. This is not an arcane science book. This book is about discovering the peace and power that lies within all of us. We'll just have a lot more fun getting to that place than your peers will have grinding through another day. Before we move any further, you should know that there are no instructions to follow, nor are there any lesson plans or management models in this book. This book is for effortless leadership. Why would we give you a list of onerous tasks?

Let's dive in.

Understand Your Processing Power

You may already know that there are two distinct levels to our brain, which we'll call the conscious and unconscious minds. Did you know that your unconscious mind processes information at 11,200,000 bits per second? If you're not a computer scientist, this may not mean much to you. But you should know that, from this fact alone, you are nothing short of a miracle in shoes. There are only a few computers ever invented that even come close to this processing power. IBM's Watson might best you, but the smartphone in your pocket has nothing on your unconscious. The conscious mind, which comprises your awareness, is vastly different. It moves at a comparative snail's pace of about 60 bits per second.

Before you get down on your conscious mind, we should give credit where credit is due. Even though it only works at 60 bits per second, it may actually be the coolest piece of tech in the modern world. Without the conscious mind, we would not be able to experience any of the beauty in life. It's our conscious mind that allows us to enjoy the smooth groove of a great jazz piece, or the complex flavors of an amazing meal, or the wonder of a spectacular sunset. If we didn't have a conscious mind, it would be like being at the best party of your life while laying passed out on the couch.

Sometimes, you might feel like you actually are just passed out on the couch in your own life. Have you ever felt like you're being guided by impulses, patterns, and emotions you don't understand? You're probably not crazy. It makes perfect sense once you know that your conscious awareness is 200,000 times slower than your unconscious mind. Don't let this scare you too much. Your brain is just trying to run an efficient organization, and it doesn't need to let your conscious mind know every detail.

To truly comprehend the rest of this book you will need to fully understand the enormous disparity between the processing speed of the two levels of mind. Use your 60 bits to ponder the tremendous implications. Consider the possibility that knowing this one data point could alter the entire way you see the world and operate in it. Does a sense of wonder arise when you consider this possibility, or do you notice fear popping up? Keep your conscious mind tuned in: Examining this insight may change the way you look at yourself, your business, and your life.

Storytellers

Dutch professor Ap Dijksterhuis, a thought leader on thought itself and the bestselling author of *The Smart Unconscious*, provides what is perhaps our favorite metaphor for visualizing how the two parts of our brain work together. Dijksterhuis brilliantly explains that our unconscious brain is like a gigantic factory with 200,000 workers. Standing in front of the factory is a reporter. We know that our conscious brain, the reporter, is not very well informed, given its processing limitations. To compensate for these limitations, it makes up all kinds of stories about what is happening in the factory. Just like a television reporter, he feels the need to explain what is going on like he knows all the facts. And, what's even worse, the reporter thinks that he is the CEO and that he controls everything that is happening in the factory. The reporter actually believes his own story and that he can control all 200,000 workers! He has no idea that he is simply a storyteller.

Thankfully, the latest research from the

field of neuroscience gives us a much clearer understanding of the relationship between the unconscious brain and the conscious brain – our storyteller. This groundbreaking research states that the unconscious brain does everything, and only afterward do we become aware of it. So, in a way, we are always living a fraction of a second in the past.

How are you sitting right now? Interestingly, as soon as your attention is brought to your posture, the reporter probably starts to explain why you are sitting the way you are. But notice that this only happens after your awareness is brought to your posture. Are the reasons the reporter gave for your posture accurate? No! In reality, it is impossible for the conscious mind to understand the complexity of decision-making occurring deeper within your brain. But that does not stop it from making up a story to explain it. Everything you do, everything you think, and every choice you make has all been determined by the factory, and afterward the reporter works to fit it into a narrative. We are like football announcers constantly commenting on the game, while at the same time believing that the game is happening thanks to our commentary.

The Muppets

Do you remember the two characters in The Muppet Show that sat up in the balcony? They constantly commented on everything that was happening on the stage. That's right, Statler and Waldorf! Just like the reporter in your head they have all types of commentary and stories about what is happening on the stage.

Now, imagine you are sitting in a movie theater. You're peacefully relaxed as you watch the movie unfold, scene by scene. As the story plays out you experience a whole collection of emotions. At times you are excited or scared, sometimes you laugh, and other times you feel deep sadness. Because you experience all of these emotions without resistance, self-judgment, or analysis, it feels wonderful. That's why you came to the movie in the first place! Isn't it interesting that people actually pay for horror movies to get frightened out of their minds? Or, they'll happily say, "I cried like a baby during that movie." Why do we do this? Because when we experience the emotions with no resistance we actually enjoy the experience.

Let's go back to our Muppets in the balcony for a quick look at how they experience the movie:

"Watch out, Bra•!"

"I knew that was going to happen, man!"

"Great, now you're in jail, you i•iot!"

"What if this en•s ba•ly?"

"What if he •oesn't manage to escape?"

"By the way, check out his shirt, it's way too tight."

"Right? He probably shrunk it in the •ryer."

"You think he has a •ryer at home?"

"You shoul• hang a shirt like that to •ry on a line, it works better."

"Or he coul• have bought a larger size."

"But anyway, he shoul∙ have staye∙ in Tibet!"

"Yes, but that girl ∙i∙ run away with his frien∙. Why ∙oes this always happen to him?"

"He shoul∙ have been frien∙lier in the beginning."

Due to the Muppets' senseless drivel, you can no longer enjoy the movie. You may even end up shouting, "Could you please quiet down?! You're ruining the entire movie!"

Sounds familiar? We have this Muppets-style dialogue running in our minds almost constantly. Our brains are chattering endlessly, creating stories and coming up with opinions on events both real and imagined. These voices provide humans with the evolutionary benefits of analysis, projecting the future, and applying old information to novel situations. But they are just broadcasts from the reporter, and when we believe every story the reporter drops into our consciousness, unwelcome things begin to happen in our mind and lives. Understanding what our mind is doing frees us from listening to the Muppets and the commentary that takes us away from being present in the moment.

Cognitive Dissonance

We all have convictions, ideas, and opinions about ourselves. When the factory does something that contradicts the views we have about ourselves, the reporter comes up with a story to make us feel better. It means that we try to justify our actions by creating a story expressly designed to make us feel better about our choice.

Let's use the example of getting into top physical condition. Most people can relate to trying to improve their health at one point or another because we believe it will make us happier or able to operate more effectively. Still, our actions often don't line up with this "believed" thought. At night when you automatically find yourself walking to the refrigerator and taking out the cookies and chocolate, the reporter might show up with his commentary:

"You can't eat vegetables all of the time, you have to have some balance!"

"You have to enjoy life an• live a little!"

"I'll just have half a bowl tonight an• eat only healthy foo•s for the rest of the week."

"I exercise• yester•ay, so it's fine."

The next day, the good intentions to skip dessert the rest of the week seem distant. Your brain might highlight that you ate mostly healthy food the day before despite your evening slip up, providing wiggle room to give yourself a pass on those big diet and exercise plans. This is partially because the reporter in our head has a tendency to adjust memories, which make our thoughts about the past subjective and unreliable. A few days later when you go to remember that night, you'll be remembering the memory, not the night itself. This is how events and situational truths can be so easily distorted, and why two people can have remarkably different accounts of the same event.

Once you fully understand both cognitive dissonance and the distorted quality of memory, you will experience every conversation in a totally different way. It will help you see through people's stories, and you might even start to laugh at your own.

Opposite Statements

Another form of easily recognizable cognitive dissonance is a concept we call "opposite statements." Say you heard someone say, unprompted, "I was really sad about the breakup with my girlfriend, but I'm over it now." No, he's not! It would never occur to him to say anything like this if the pain of the breakup wasn't still at the forefront of his mind. I witnessed this firsthand not long ago when my dad looked out of the window and said, "It's another rainy day, but I'm not letting my mood depend on the weather." Clearly, his mood had been affected by the weather, and his words were a response to that. If someone isn't bothered by something, they wouldn't mention it. Imagine you are visiting a friend that has music on. You would never say: "I don't mind that the music is on." It would simply not appear in your awareness. You would only say something if the music was bothering you. This is the reporter doing sloppy justification work and trying to convince itself that whatever is happening is, in fact, in alignment with the story it's telling.

In my private coaching practice, I encountered opposite statements constantly. Whenever a high-powered CEO would tell me he wasn't going to drink that night, I knew the chances were extremely high that he would. Someone that isn't grappling with self-control around alcohol wouldn't feel compelled to say something like that. They just wouldn't drink, sans commentary. The chances that the factory produces a martini in his hand is incredibly high, despite what the reporter has to say. The same goes for watching porn, overeating, shopping, or any other behavior that feels uncontrollable and impulsive. Recognizing opposite statements provides insights for tuned-in leaders. If the leader is awake to how the reporter works, he or she can be more aware of the unconscious mind's habits and desires and can better predict future actions.

Colored Glasses

The reporter obviously doesn't have the full picture about what's happening inside the factory. And, as it turns out, the factory workers are only able to see the rest of the world through the distorted windows of the building. So by the time information about the broader world goes through your unconscious and gets to your conscious mind, you're seeing a heavily edited reality.

It's like going through life wearing colored glasses. You see the world through your own filters, and what you see is never objective. These colored glasses are permanently attached to your face, but there may be a time when you become aware that you are wearing them. When this realization hits you, you inevitably discover that none of your thoughts and opinions are true. Not one of them! They are only true for you. There is nothing right or wrong about these colored glasses, but effortless, enlightened leadership requires that you know you are wearing them and that everyone else is too. These glasses will never come off and we will never be able to look at the world with complete objectivity. By knowing this, the enlightened leader is less identified with their own thoughts, ideas, and opinions, and is more open-minded and capable of truly innovative thinking. This leader encourages humility, respect, and openness among their team, as this insight leads people to value their peers' unique, subjective contributions (as well as their own) and to listen before asserting their own rigid truth.

Some of your team's "unique" contributions might seem utterly foreign to you, but you can learn to glean the value from other perspectives without your loud judgments getting in the way. For instance, let's say that someone opens a meeting by proposing that bananas are the best fruit. Perhaps you love bananas. But I don't. What does that say about bananas? Nothing. A banana is simply a banana. Every opinion we have about bananas comes from subjective thoughts, and the same is true about the oddball idea you overheard in your last meeting. Your personal reaction might be instructive, but you shouldn't forget that you are bringing your subjective vision to the table, not the ultimate truth about the idea's viability. By holding your opinions lightly, you can more effectively consider ideas outside of your norm.

Shortcuts

As we have just learned, we are storytellers who are full of cognitive dissonance and opposite statements and see the world through reality-distorting glasses. But, wait...there's more. Our brains are also shortcut-creating machines. Please take two seconds to think of a famous movie star.

Done?

Let's assume you chose Brad Pitt. Why did you choose him? Your brain certainly didn't go through every movie star you have ever known. It  simply created a shortcut and Brad's name shows up. Now, think of a city in the United States. Instantly one comes to your mind. Let's say it was Chicago. Your brain didn't go through every city you know in the U.S. It went to Chicago effortlessly.

The brain creates shortcuts to save energy. It's like we all have a filing cabinet in our head with a label on the front of each door. In one file cabinet you have all of the movie stars you know, but "Brad Pitt" is written on the label. Marketers take advantage of this tendency to make shortcuts by exposing people to repetitive messages that connect a category to a specific brand, such as McDonald's for fast food. Some brands and products have even become synonymous in common speech; you might say you're buying "a coke" even if you're not buying Coca-Cola specifically. Marketers are, in essence, naming your filing cabinets for you.

This is a tendency to be aware of, as these shortcuts inform our opinions and allow us to come to conclusions based on limited information and analysis. What is your opinion of Steve Jobs? Your brain can come up with an opinion about Steve Jobs in a millisecond, even though you could never go through all of the information you have ever heard about Steve Jobs, much less all of the information there is to know about Steve Jobs. Your brain creates a shortcut and says he's either crazy, brilliant, or whatever trait you read about him once in a magazine. You probably don't even remember where you came across the information or why you feel the way you do. Knowing that our opinions are created by our tendency for shortcutting, we can get less attached to our opinions and be more open-minded as we become aware of our subjective nature.

Subjectivity, as you might have guessed, is dependent on there being a "subject". But with everything we know about the workers in our mind, can we say who that subject is, really? Your intuitions and assumptions might be monumentally wrong.

Let's explore how our brains create and relate to this subject.

CHAPTER

02
The Clouds

Self-Awareness

When you look in a mirror what do you see? YOU, right? But what happens when a dog looks in a mirror? What does it see and how does it react? Well, it sees another dog. If you have a dog, put him in front of a mirror and observe his reaction. Some dogs start to bark while others actually attack the mirror. Particularly inquisitive dogs might look behind the mirror to see if there is another dog. The dog has consciousness; it is aware of the sight of another dog. But it does not understand that the reflection in the mirror is its own. So why do humans see ourselves in the mirror but a dog does not see himself? It's very simple, humans have self-awareness and dogs do not. As a matter of fact, only a scant few species in the world have been found to be capable of self-awareness, including humans, dolphins, elephants, gorillas, chimpanzees, orangutans – and strangely enough – magpies.

The Dog And The Cat

Self-awareness changes everything about the way one considers their actions. If a dog sees a cat, it will probably chase the cat. As the dog runs towards the cat, the cat instinctively scales the nearest tree to escape danger. The dog will sit below the tree and bark for a while before it loses interest and goes back home. Now imagine you, and not your dog, see a cat in your yard and you want to chase it away. You run toward it and the cat again climbs into a tree for safety. At this point, you feel annoyed at your failure to get the cat out of your yard. You consider your options and decide to head back to the house. The difference between you and the dog in this example is that you are able to see yourself in the third person and look at your own actions as if from a remote location. The dog only has awareness of the cat and the situation as it unfolds in each moment. He doesn't have the self-awareness to think thoughts like: "I just chased a really fast cat." "What is wrong with me that I couldn't catch that lousy cat?" "I guess I am just not good enough to catch cats." "I need some therapy to figure out what my problem is because I feel terrible about myself."

18 Months

For about the first year-and-a-half of your life, you only have awareness. A child is aware of other people and the environment, but does not see itself as an "I". If you place a one-year-old child in front of a mirror, it will be aware of the reflection but it doesn't yet realize it is looking at him or herself. Then, after approximately 18 months, the child suddenly thinks, "Hey, that reflection is ME!" From this moment on, the reporter inside of our head creates the "I" thought. Self-awareness is born, which is the conscious knowledge of one's own character, feelings, motives, and desires. It is also often referred to as the "ego". In Sanskrit, it is called Ahamkara, which literally means the "I-creator".

When a thought arises, the brain creates the idea, "I think." When a feeling arises, the brain creates the idea, "I feel." When a choice is made, the brain creates the idea, "I choose." You breathe continuously, so the brain creates the idea, "I am breathing." Blood moves through your veins all day, but the brain thinks, "My blood is moving through my body." Self-awareness ensures that we see ourselves as an individual. Almost everything that happens or occurs to you reinforces the idea that "I" exists.

This Is My Ball

After that critical turning point around 18 months of age, the MY identity is installed for life for most of us. A ball is not a just a ball anymore, it is MY ball. The child starts to see everything through this filter of MY. Something is either mine or not mine. "This is MY doll. This is MY toy car. This is not MY gum, it's yours." Later in life, you start to claim other things through the MY lens. "This is MY money. This is MY country. This is MY partner." And the illusion gets more solid. Most people never develop their minds beyond the observation of their one-and-half-year-old self. But if you are still reading, we will presume you are seeking greater understanding of "you" and how that "you" functions in your life, relationships, and business.

The Functional I-Idea

Our brains do not create these "I" thoughts for no reason. They are necessary for our survival. Even though the "I" is merely a thought and a feeling, it is undeniably functional in our daily lives. When you are thirsty, you say, "May I have a drink of water?" You don't say, "This body is thirsty." And when you suddenly have a good idea, you say, "I have a really good idea." You don't say, "This brain has generated a really good idea." It's perfectly normal and useful to use the pronoun "I" in our daily lives. You don't have to get rid of your "I"– life just becomes more relaxed if you see it as a functional tool and not as reality.

Your internal reporter is especially keen on this "I" framing since it gives your 60-bit conscious mind a concept to orient itself around. It's a convenient story, but it is not ultimate reality. Let's not be too hard on ourselves for believing this illusion, though. Everyone you encounter also believes the "I" thought. Our whole society is designed around the thought of being a separate person! People have been calling us

"Scott" or "Paul" for decades, so why would we ever question who we are?

How can we know that this "I" isn't as solid as we thought? If our concept of "I" is just a tool, who are we, really? A simple thought experiment makes it clear.

Who Are You?

Normally, when you ask people who they are, they will tell you their name. But if you change your name, are you still you? Yes, you are. Clearly, you are not your name. Next, people tend to point to their bodies. But if you were to lose both of your arms and legs, are you still you? Yes, people reply. So, where is this "I" hidden inside of your body? Is it located in your heart, your kidneys, your spine, or even your brain? Some will say, my "I" is located in my heart. But, if you were to have a heart transplant would you still be you? The scientific consensus is yes. Others will point to their head like the I is located somewhere inside of their brain. Neuroscientists have employed all of the latest science to locate the internal I, but it is nowhere to be found. There is no puppet inside of your brain that is controlling the steering wheel. All there is is an amazing process that involves 100 billion neurons making more than 100 trillion connections, making possible the illusion of an I.

Einstein described this "I" sensation we have as a

trick occurring in our conscious minds:

A human being is a part of the whole, called by us 'Universe' — a part limited in time and space. He experiences himself, his thoughts, and feelings as something separated from the rest, a kind of optical illusion of his consciousness.

– Albert Einstein

A Cloud Is Born

Much of our brain's activity is optimized to help us survive the social and environmental conditions from thousands of years past. It's not surprising that so many live confused, frustrating lives in our modern times. Much of what our brain instinctively scans the environment for is not in alignment with the realities of our times. Due to this confusion, stressful thoughts arise that act much like clouds in the sky. Sometimes these thoughts are beautiful, light, wispy clouds that pass quickly and cause no upset. Other thoughts develop into dark, ominous clouds that block the power of the sun and create a feeling of heaviness and misery. These are the clouds we will be focusing on for the remainder of the book.

As we progress through our development, we begin to work harder to pick the right clothes, say the right things, and, in more recent times, have the right personal brand on social media. We construct our self-image around a critical survival mechanism: making sure people like us.

We have deep-seated, biologically driven fears of not fitting in and not being good enough.

For many, this fear is reinforced from a young age and used for the sake of discipline. "Put that thing down, you should have known better!" your parents might have said. "Why can't you be more like your sister! What's wrong with you?" The message is clear: You aren't good as you ought to be, and you need to constantly watch yourself and punish yourself. Your brain generates a fear that you are always at risk of being a no-good, useless human that others could toss aside at any moment.

The fear of being useless has been driven so deeply into our subconscious mind that our whole life becomes oriented around managing this dark cloud. It doesn't help that everywhere we look we seem to see perfection portrayed in others. On television, in magazines, and on our social feeds, we see beautiful, seemingly happy people. The phenomenon of social media-induced depression is becoming an increasingly popular area of study for psychological researchers. As people see the highly edited and most joyous moments of other people's lives, they are increasingly critical and ashamed of their own comparatively dull experience. Since we carry around the illusion of being a separate ME – combined with the fear that we aren't good enough and will be rejected – it's perfectly reasonable that we compare ourselves to the images we see and try to determine exactly where and how our lives are lacking.

And so we begin to wonder: "Why don't I look

like this? What is wrong with me? She is so beautiful and I have all of this acne!" You begin to obsess over the image you see in the mirror. You see imperfections in your skin and body that look different than the happy, healthy, smiling image you saw of your old classmate on a trip to Monaco. Unfortunately, your mind is not developed in a way that assists you in seeing through all of the images in the media. You are not aware that nearly everything has been photoshopped or manipulated to smooth out imperfections, and you're not aware of the countless other moments where that person is lonely, sad, or bored. You begin to identify with your seeming ugliness and inadequacy. You see your nose as too big. You think your legs are too short and your one crooked tooth is embarrassing. You decide you're not as adventurous, intelligent, or fulfilled as everyone else seems to be. And here is where the distorted self-image is born. You have now entered the prison of your own mind. You have convinced yourself that you ARE as bad as you FEEL, and you certainly don't feel good enough.

The more the reporter spins this story, the more

often it gets encoded in the programming of our unconscious minds, carving deeper and deeper ditches for the river of our thoughts to flow through. Self-loathing becomes a pattern of our operating system. Becoming aware of your own mind and understanding this process can act as an antidote.

Identification

No form of success or achievement is a lasting solution to our fear of inadequacy. Each promotion only brings temporary relief; each good grade or completed project or successful networking event is just a band-aid. Our brain adapts to its environment. When you step into a hot jacuzzi, the temperature feels wonderful. But after a few minutes, you're used to it. You adjust your standards for what an "exceptional" temperature (or career or grade) looks like. No matter how successful you are, how much attention you get, or how much money you own, you will get used to it in no time.

The very thought of being an independent "I" means that the impulse toward striving and dissatisfaction will always be there. When you see yourself as a separate individual it gives rise to comparison. You identify as a separate self and instinctively judge this self against the others you see, giving rise to feelings of inadequacy and the compulsion to control and change yourself. Some part of you fears it will never be enough.

And that part is right. It won't.

It's not because you aren't working hard enough; it's because the entire premise is wrong. Even the most successful leaders and entrepreneurs are often driven by this fear, not realizing the productivity and impact they could achieve if they understood the nature of their own mind and could free themselves from their own mental prisons of self-identification and the "I" concept.

Dominating And Pleasing

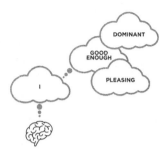

When an "I" goes to solve its problem of never being good enough, two approaches present themselves: trying to dominate people or trying to please people. Dominant behavior is all about proving to the world that you are worthy by being aggressive, pushy, and seeking conflict. Essentially, the dominant personality seeks to elevate him- or herself by bringing others down. Jealousy and greed are often emotions that accompany this type of behavior. It's not hard to spot this type of person. There's likely someone within your own company that overpowers their colleagues in meetings, loudly sharing their own thoughts while giving others little space to respond or voice their own views. You might be this person. And you might already be aware that you are compensating for the fundamental fear that you aren't good enough.

On the other side of the spectrum, the conflict-avoidant take a different approach to combat their fears. Pleasers seek attention and validation by constantly responding to the whims of others. Pleasers tend to suppress their opinions and feelings to avoid offending others or risking social backlash.

It's easy to observe the dynamic between these behavioral types within relationships: One person starts to act in a dominant way while the other reverts to the role of the pleaser in order to avoid conflict, negative emotion, and relationship-damaging consequences. This dynamic leaves both parties trapped in fear and in unproductive behavioral loops. In the end, both pleasing and dominating are dead-end streets. Neither solve the underlying problem nor do they allow for the experience of effortless living. While truly solving for the problem of our perceived inadequacy seems more difficult than staying within our habits of dominating or pleasing, in reality, it takes a huge amount of energy to operate from either of these modes of behavior, both of which create colossal messes in our lives in the meantime.

Relax, Nothing Is Under Control

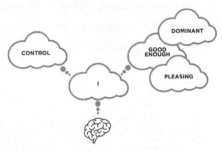

Now, let's take a closer look at the other dark cloud that rules the typical person's life: the need for control. From infancy, we were taught to control ourselves and take responsibility for our actions. This doesn't, on its face, seem like a particularly horrible concept. But do we actually have control of anything?

You were born on a certain date, to certain parents, in a certain period of history, within a certain country and culture. Did you have any control over this? You grew up within a neighborhood with certain kids that became your friends. Did you pick the neighborhood and friends? You happened to go to a particular school and have particular teachers when you were young. Did you control this? These examples barely scratch the surface of the circumstances that make up your life, and yet even these few factors have an enormous impact on how you think, speak, and behave today. And, you didn't choose or control any of them! They all just happened the way they happened. How about your genes, your natural talents, your voice, your looks? Any control? No! Do you choose to move your blood through your veins? Do you choose to grow your hair? Do you choose when you get hungry or tired or have to go to the bathroom? Do you choose how you feel? If people could choose how they feel, everyone would be happy, joyous, and free every second of the day. The statistics show a different reality.

The way your life is going depends on millions of factors over which you have absolutely no control. If ten years ago someone had shown you a short video about what your life looks like today, would it have matched your predictions? The same unpredictability holds true for the next ten years, despite valiant attempts at strategic planning for your department or goal-setting with your spouse. When you face a situation, your brain can churn out any number of scenarios about what will happen. But the most likely option of all is that what happens won't remotely fit into the scenarios you crafted and that variables beyond your awareness will determine the ultimate course of events.

When you are watching a movie, you realize that everything in the movie goes as it is supposed to and will happen regardless of your response. Therefore, there is no reason to worry. Every single scene will simply be what it will be. Imagine that everything was like this: that you don't have to worry about anything at all; that everything you do and all the choices you make all happen by themselves. In that case, you've never done anything wrong, and you can leave the feelings of guilt, anxiety, stress, and frustration behind. Doesn't that sound wonderful?

Let's look deeper. Who is in control of your thoughts, actions, and feelings? It's not the "you" in your awareness - it's the factory! The reporter is scrambling to create a story about the flurry of activity happening in your conscious mind, without the ability to see or understand the massive complexity happening deeper within the building. Then he or she is simply reading a press release stating that you are in control and are intentionally guiding every single one of your own behaviors and emotions. Because of this trick, it is our experience that we are the one creating our thoughts and feelings and that we are choosing our actions.

Meanwhile, while we are falling for the trick, everything is simply playing out as it does.

Life is what happens to you while you are busy making other plans.

- John Lennon

Frustration, Fear, Guilt, Blame, And Overwhelm

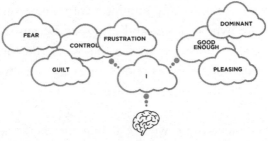

When things go differently than we desire we feel out of control and a new cloud starts to appear: frustration! We think, "This is not what I wanted. This isn't the way it should be. Why is this happening to me? Why won't my team cooperate?" Without a doubt, it's the frustration cloud that arises most frequently for people. For some, almost every hour. This feeling of frustration spawns even more thoughts – mainly about the past – of how things should have gone differently. Then the downward spiral is triggered. A fear cloud starts to form as the "I" starts to worry about the future and everything that can go wrong. You begin to worry that things will not turn out the way you want and visualize scenarios of failure and abandonment.

This is the terrifying place where so many of us spend our time.

Think of the last time you were lying awake in bed with anxious thoughts. Typically, the cloud-filled mind will lay there with all kinds of projections and horrible scenarios about what might happen in the future. And since it is late at night and your tired conscious mind is not guarding the rest of the brain against these crazy ideas, the thoughts can spin out of control. From here, additional clouds of guilt, blame, and shame form. Since we believe we are in control, every bad thing that happens or any emotion that arises that we don't approve of is an inexcusable failure. Finding this idea unbearable, we then try to solve for this guilt and shame by creating the idea that it really wasn't our fault. It was "their" fault. And, just like clockwork, a blame cloud forms. It's all so predictable. Meanwhile, in reality, things continue to simply happen as they happen.

Stress

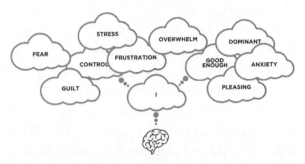

It's no surprise that living our personal and professional lives with all of these clouds, endless projections, and worrying thoughts leads to enormous amounts of stress and tension. It's from this place that mental suffering starts to take over, overwhelm rears its ugly head, and burnout becomes a way of being. From here, we begin to live emotion to emotion and mental chaos takes over. You might hear a voice in your head shouting, "I just can't take it anymore!"

But who is the "I" that can't take it anymore?

Escaping The Clouds

As we struggle to keep our heads above the flood of stress and negativity, we are highly motivated to search for a solution to the pain. We try to find relief from our suffering in getting all of the material stuff we think will solve our problems. And so we buy a new car, or a new work gadget, or maybe even a new house. This might really work for a while. The endorphins that are produced in the brain are unmistakably an effective tool in dispersing the painful clouds. Eventually, the very thought of buying something new triggers endorphin production and builds an increasingly addicting pattern. But, unsurprisingly, after a few hours, the clouds begin to pop back up again. So the only solution is to buy more! And more, and more - even if you already don't have the money to pay off your credit card bills as it is. We'll even borrow money to experience these powerful, relaxing brain chemicals. It's simply biology playing out its natural functions. It's like comedian George Carlin said: We have "taken this beautiful place and turned it into what it is today – a shopping mall." The world is full of shopping addicts looking to erase the clouds in their minds. But eventually, we begin to realize that shopping isn't a long-term solution. Hopefully this happens before you go bankrupt.

But that's only the beginning of the strategies the mind has to ward off the clouds. Enter the likes of beer and chocolate. A few beers can have the effect of quieting the neocortex and slowing down the worrying thoughts. Many try to escape the clouds by taking a daily dose of alcohol. It's not surprising that about 13 percent of the U.S. population has an alcohol problem. Others use recreational drugs to suppress their mental suffering, while 13 percent of Americans are on prescription antidepressants. Chocolate is another potent salve. Eating gives us momentary relief as our 60 bits of consciousness focus on the delicious food and the worrying thoughts abate. And so we eat and we eat. In 2015, nine percent of the U.S. population had diabetes, and this number is increasing. More people die these days from too much food than from a lack of food.

While we're munching on candy at our desk, it

might occur to us that if we could just get the right job or hire the perfect team, everything would be alright. It's so common to come across the person that is incredibly stressed by their 70-hour work weeks and is convinced that the promotion on the horizon will free them from their suffering. So they exhaust themselves for years and eventually get that promotion. And it works! The clouds disappear. But again, only for a little while. Here is where many people make a mistake in judgment: They think that the reason the clouds disappeared was because they got the new job or position. In reality, it is the freedom from desire that produced this newfound relaxation, not the new job itself. Maybe the Buddha was on to something! Nonetheless, the clouds eventually reappear. Nothing has really changed.

After years of doing whatever they can to get rid of those pesky clouds they think they see a way out: Hire a life coach or a therapist. They'll have the answer! In many cases this can be the desperate act that finally leads to some relief, but probably not for the reason they were expecting.

Yes, seeking out this professional help can provide an opportunity to step back, take a deep look at their lives, the patterns they repeat, and all of the clouds they carry around. But even this doesn't make the clouds actually go away.

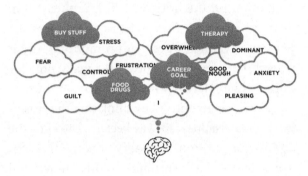

How To Get Rid Of The Clouds?

Just becoming aware of the clouds in your mind during a therapy session doesn't necessarily bring insight into the clouds' true nature or fundamental cause. Where do all of these clouds come from? Where do they exist?

Inside your head! And, notably, nowhere else.

So how many of these thought clouds are actually true?

None.

All of these clouds are merely illusions appearing in your mind in response to any number of unconscious processes. Even the thought of a YOU or an "I" is an illusion your mind creates. Once you realize you are not an I, that you simply exist as you are, the fear of not being good enough starts to dissolve, as well as the defense mechanisms of dominating and pleasing. Once you realize that everything goes as it goes, as well as your thoughts, emotions, choices, and feelings, then the stress of needing to control your life also dissolves. The worried mind can become calm or even disappear altogether. And so with all the escape routes of buying stuff, boozing, overeating, or ladder-climbing.

CHAPTER

The Cloudless Mind

From A Worried Mind To
A Functional Mind

All clouds consist of feelings and emotions. The typical human has between 30,000 and 60,000 thoughts per day, and approximately 95 percent of them are thoughts of worry. You do not create your thoughts, they simply arise. Thoughts are like clouds passing by in the sky. They show up, hang around for a bit and move along. When you learn to distinguish which thoughts are useful and which are not, you can enter a space of ease and effortlessness.

There are, of course, useful thoughts. For example, "I need to go shopping for food so I can eat tonight," would be a quite useful thought. Or, "Did I feed the dog? Did I water the plants? Where did I park my car?" In addition to their practical utility, functional thoughts can be very pleasant. They enable us to time travel, for instance. We can access memories that we enjoy or we can look forward to having dinner with our partner next weekend. We can even have functional thoughts about things that we want to change. Through this, we make plans, we create goals, and we schedule our actions. These are very functional and increase our odds of survival.

Now let's take a closer look at the worried, stressed mind and how it is different from the functional, effortless mind.

Worried Mind	Functional Mind
Problems	Solutions
Difficulties	Possibilities
This will never end	This is only temporary
Rigid	Flexible
Tense	Relax
Stressed	Effortless

People who have obsessive, anxious thoughts can cultivate a calmer mind by realizing: "Oh, that's just another thought." By understanding that you do not create your thoughts, you can look at them and stop believing them. When this insight is integrated into your daily life, you automatically distinguish between functional and worrying thoughts. It's amazing how quickly useless thoughts disappear once you simply observe them like passing clouds and recognize their baselessness.

Emotions

Thoughts create emotions and emotions create thoughts. Understanding this is important, as much of our life is spent trying to create the emotions we think we want. The problem is, our brain doesn't know the difference between reality and the fictions we create. If you have lost your keys, an emotion instantly pops up. The same emotion, however, occurs when you think you have lost your keys. It's your thoughts that create the stress, not the situation itself.

Not only do we take our thoughts of worry as truth, we take our emotions gravely seriously. Whenever we experience an emotion like frustration, the worried mind will tell you that it will last forever. While in reality, if it is seen for what it really is - just a thought - it will disappear in minutes. An emotion is nothing more than a cloud passing by. But as we identify with the emotion by thinking, "This is MY emotion," we begin to focus on the emotion, add meaning to it, and try to control it - ultimately making it bigger and bigger.

Generalizing

The worried mind says: This happens to me all the time.

The functional mind says: *This can happen sometimes.*

The worried mind says: *People can't be truste*.

The functional mind says: *That person can't be truste*.

The worried mind says: *This will last forever.*

The functional mind says: *This will pass soon.*

As the worried mind generalizes, it starts to think it has to fight the situation and that it has to fight itself. These are the moments when you are lying awake in bed in terror. A worry-thought comes up, and instantly the next worry-thought tries to get rid of that first thought. But it doesn't work, and so a third thought comes up, spiraling you into a storm of suffering.

Imagine a still lake. A thought or an emotion is like a small stone that enters the water, which creates a ripple effect. How can you go back to the still water? By doing nothing. But the worried mind wants to get rid of the ripple and throws another stone, which creates another ripple. In the end, there are a thousand stones in the water and you are dealing with chaotic waves inside your head.

Collaboration With Clouds

Leading teams of people that are full of clouds makes communication, collaboration, and change exceedingly difficult. How could they be open to change and to innovation? Since they are filled with fear, frustration, guilt, stress, tension, and mental suffering, achieving these goals is a painful struggle. This is where real leadership comes into play. The effortless modern leader has a deep understanding of the nature of these clouds and can address them more effectively. If a leader is not liberated from his or her own clouds, they tend to throw extra clouds upon their team in an attempt to control them. This is what we call "managing others." It's unnatural for our brains to be managed in this way. Our evolutionary history shows us why.

The Savannah Brain

Much of the functioning of our brains evolved from our time as hunter-gatherers in the brutal environment of the African savannah. To survive, we formed ourselves into groups of about 150 people. From here we would establish a system of trust that facilitated all of our survival needs. Within the group, leaders would naturally arise. In general, the leaders were the ones with the highest skill level in the area most critical to the group's survival. If you had the ability to execute the task at hand better than anyone else, you would naturally gain followers who benefitted from your skill and example. Typically, leaders were older members of the group that had years of experience in their respective discipline. They also tended to be the most physically strong. They were always present and visible to the group. This familiarity instilled trust as others observed his actions and felt confident about his ability to hold the long-term vision for the group. In addition to their talents, experience, passion, and integrity, they were almost always the most charismatic and energetic. It was absolutely critical to inspire the group members to stay positive and proactive in these harsh times.

Back on the savannah, leaders were highly respected and revered. But if the concept of a manager would have been introduced, this manager likely would have been killed instantly. Imagine what it would have been like for a hunter to have some guy running along beside him telling him what to do, how to do it, and when the deadline was. Think what it would have been like if there was someone whose sole responsibility was to assess your hunting KPIs, evaluate your tool-making effectiveness through a scoring system, and pass judgment on your adherence to the vision. This sort of management just grows the clouds by forcing you to constantly monitor whether you are good enough and whether everything is under control. Our brains are designed to have inspirational leadership that enables cloud-free, autonomous action, not management that inhibits us from freely pursuing the task at hand.

Taking Away The Mental Sludge

The clouds are the mental sludge we have on top of our natural programming. When we take away this mental sludge, we can operate naturally and freely. The modern leader understands that we are all uniquely programmed human beings, and, convicted in this knowledge, he or she leads insightfully. They understand that where there is an "I" there will always be clouds. And most importantly, that they must be aware of their own unique programming and clouds. If the leader fails to do the work of identifying their own clouds, they will fall into the same trap that is affecting his followers. Many leaders unwittingly project all of their compensating behavior on those they lead. Unexamined, the asleep leader operates from a place of dominating or pleasing which ultimately leads to fear, frustration, and stress throughout the organization. From here the leader looks to exercise dominating control and the cycle of blame and pain starts up. The enlightened leader knows the amount of energy that this cloud behavior consumes and is willing to do whatever is necessary to avoid it.

As a leader, it is imperative that you help your people understand their clouds. When the leader sees people struggling to be good enough, he will operate as a mirror and demonstrate a powerful alternative. If someone acts in a dominant way to get confirmation and attention, the leader will help this person become aware of its effect on the team. If someone is pleasing and looking to be validated, the leader will support this person in speaking up, setting their boundaries, and ending the suppression of their feelings.

When it comes to the cloud of "control", the leader will help people to separate worry- based thoughts from functional thoughts. When something happens, just ask yourself:

Can I change it?

If not: then let it be.	It is out of your control so there is no use worrying.
If yes: then change it.	Use your functional thoughts to change it.

Trust

During the time that we lived on the savannah, danger was ever-present. It could be the weather, wild animals, human enemies, or basic lack of resources. As an added stressor, we were physically outmatched by the ferocious power of the lions and cheetahs that saw us as prey. But we managed to survive quite nicely thanks to our neocortex. It was our superior intelligence that provided us with the power to evaluate and make sense of the hostile environment in order to survive. Our brains came up with powerful inventions that vaulted us to the top of the food chain in a relatively short period of time. While inventions such as spears and clubs were extremely useful to help us defend ourselves and to hunt, they were not the only reason our survival odds increased. It was our powerful ability to organize and collaborate that proved a greater tool than any material object we created. And the basis of every collaboration is trust.

Say I went out to hunt animals for food while you were assigned the task of finding water for the group. We would have to trust that each of us would return in the evening with our task accomplished. In order for each of us to be most effective in our own job, we needed to have full faith that the others would be effective in theirs. We also had to trust that our other group members would share the fruits of their labor. Without this trust, there would be no possibility of survival. This trust was extended to each member of the group as the combination of everyone's skills was essential to simply stay alive.

As soon as the clouds come in, trust decreases. If you feel that people are manipulative or overloaded with frustration or with fear, it has a negative effect on the connection we feel. Would you trust a leader that is inauthentic, dishonest, scared, stressed, and frustrated? Probably not. In order to gain trust, people must feel you are genuine.

Authenticity

If someone tries to be something he or she is not, you can instantly feel it. When someone is insecure and acts in a dominant or pleasing way, they become inauthentic. These manipulating ways of being are always cloud-based actions or reactions. They are simply playing out the function of the particular cloud that is most present. Once you become liberated from these clouds, authenticity and real power come through.

For some, this might be a bit scary. When people talk to you about their emotions or problems, they are often looking for confirmation. They want you to tell them that they are right and that other people are wrong. It is the reporter inside their head that is looking for support for its own stories. This is where you have the opportunity to listen and exercise compassion without taking sides and without giving in to the impulse to make them feel better. You can see that now as a cloud of pleasing that is just about trying to make that person like you.

This is when true connection can take place. Others love being with you and value your open, non-judgmental authenticity. You listen to them without a desire to overwhelm them with your opinions. You will still have own ideas and opinions, but you will maintain awareness of their subjective nature.

Creativity And Innovation

This connection and awareness make the other four critical "C" skills of the 21st century possible: critical thinking, creativity, communication, and collaboration. Since you are aware that everything you think and every idea you have is subjective and selective, you will be consistently open-minded to novel ideas. This is the basis for critical thinking, in which you can assess new ideas instead of over-identifying with your own opinions and limiting your ability to see alternatives. Communication and collaboration become much easier when people are free from the clouds, as the ego games, manipulation, and impulse to compensate dissolve. With an open, blue-sky mind, creativity automatically arises.

This peaceful, blue sky image is instructive. We tend to think of innovation as hard work that requires teeth-gritting focus. When we're in this mindset though, our brain is operating with Beta wave patterns. This brain state is characterized by intense focus, alertness, and deep concentration. In this Beta state, we are productive, but not creative. It is also the state where anxious thoughts pop up and where stress is generated.

An Alpha brain wave pattern provides a more promising state for effortless innovation. This is the state we are in when we are relaxed, during light meditation, or while daydreaming. In the Alpha state, we are not filtering information and don't have a single point of focus.

The Theta state is an interesting one. You reach this state when you are in deep meditation or in a light sleep. It is the state where you experience vivid visualizations, great inspiration, and profound creativity. You can even reach this state while showering. Perhaps you've experienced this yourself while relaxing in the warm water after a long day and suddenly becoming aware of an unexpected solution to a problem or a promising entrepreneurial idea. The Theta state also happens when you are dreaming, and we all know how creative dreams can be.

For example, I recently bought a record player

and played my old Elvis Presley records for hours. On the same day, the woman that cleans my home told me she is quitting because she had found another job. As my brain processed this information in my sleep, I dreamt that Elvis Presley was coming to clean my house. In my dream, it was totally normal for me to see Elvis Presley busy holding the vacuum cleaner in my living room, and my judging mind didn't limit the stories and connections my creative mind could generate. While this dream wasn't particularly useful at work the next day, this state of thinking without structure is paramount to creativity. And who knows, maybe an Elvis-themed cleaning service would be big business!

The ideas that arise from these states of mind are gifts from the factory. These are the stress-free moments when we are not trying to get somewhere, impress anyone, or force anything. Innovative ideas, beautiful songs, and wonderful art all come as a gift when you are in the Alpha or Theta state. Bono once said, "Do not interfere with the pen, let the pen do its work." Said another way, just relax and let the ideas flow.

Beethoven concurred with Bono. He was known to say that he had no idea where his ideas came from, they would simply appear out of nowhere. Every creative idea is a gift from the factory, not an achievement from the reporter.

A clear example that demonstrates this idea is how common it is for a band's first album to be a success and their second album to be a struggle. The first album was likely written from a totally free state of mind. It's from this freedom that true magic happens and beautiful songs are created. After the success of the first album, they were awarded a big recording contract. Now the pressure is on to repeat their success. They are given a deadline and all of the sudden the Beta state gets triggered. This is when writer's block occurs because the band is trying to write songs from a rational place, not one of creative expression. From this place, the clouds begin to gather and the brain, searching safety or seeking approval, might replicate old songs that were well-received. Or they try out a new sound that is inauthentic but seems to be what others want. The lack of authenticity is audible.

At this point, it is probably quite clear how information about your brain states can make your life easier. Whenever you have a problem to solve or you want to create something or innovate...RELAX! Often when we need to find a solution, that's when we being to stress. And stress is the end of all creativity.

Brainstorming With The Clouds

Now that we know this, let's look at the old "brainstorming session." We've all been there, sitting around a table with a bunch of people staring at notepads and drinking coffee. The leader of the company walks in and says, "This afternoon between 2 and 4 pm we are going to get super creative and come up with some really innovative ideas." In order to impress the leader and the others sitting around the table, everyone starts writing down a lot of ideas. No one wants to look like a fool and so we all try to be as productive as possible. This puts everyone in the Beta state – the state in which we are fundamentally not creative. What typically happens is that a whole bunch of stuff gets written down, but nothing truly new and creative arises. The attempt to be productive is, in this instance, counter-productive.

Not only are people at this point operating in the Beta state, but they are filled with clouds. The first person wants to dominate to prove he is good enough, so he starts interjecting his ideas. The person next to him is insecure and the thought pops up, "Man, I better come up with a great idea or I'm going to look really bad at my job!" Hastily, he puts his rational mind to work in an attempt to come up with a great idea quickly, which immediately blocks his creativity. So he brings up an idea he had months ago to say something and save face. The other insecure people in the room respond to the idea in the role of the pleaser because they don't want to hurt the poor guy's feelings. There are others in the room who don't like the way things are going and the ideas that are being presented, so they become consumed with frustration. They start to blame others for the lack of creativity at the meeting. Still more chime in with conservative ideas in order to create some sense of control. Finally, clouds of guilt and shame appear in those who are looking to compensate for past mistakes and fear making another one now. This group comes up with more useless ideas in an effort to look proactive and gain approval from the other members of the group.

A storm in the brain indeed.

The State Of Flow, The Zone

Given these insights into our brain, it's clear that we need to become masters of cultivating a new kind of focus: a calm focus. When we speak of calm focus we are referring to something akin to being in "the zone." The zone is often referred to in sports, the arts, and other areas where peak performance is observed. In the zone, one is lost in the task at hand and operates from an effortless state. One literally becomes one with whatever they are doing. This flow happens when we are in the Alpha and Theta states.

Picture any athlete you have ever observed that was in the zone. What expression is on their face? How do they walk or run? How do they react to seeming adversity? What type of energy do they give off? If you did this exercise we bet that there would be one facet that is present in all of these situations: calm. Calm denotes understanding. Calm means you can see. Calm exudes confidence. It is in these calm moments when you are in flow; when things seem to happen effortlessly.

In these moments, self-awareness is turned off and we dissolve in what we are doing at the moment. We all know these moments where we are completely absorbed in an activity - when we are captivated by reading a book, engaging in good conversation, watching a movie, making love, or playing a sport. There are moments when you are active and simultaneously experiencing an inner peace. We also experience this when we laugh, dance, or sing. The anxious mind is switched off and we are in the flow and we are 'in the now'. We are fully absorbed in an activity and there are no thoughts that give us a feeling of frustration, anxiety, or stress.

The Sandcastle

A child can get incredibly absorbed in building a sandcastle. He or she can be busy for hours, digging, adding details, and bolstering their creation. Then everything is washed away, bit by bit, until nothing is left. The child is deeply happy and enjoys every moment. It is free from worry. When we as adults lay on the beach, the Muppets in our heads are constantly chattering away:

"Yester•ay the weather was better. If only we went to the beach yester•ay..."

"I have to call back that annoying client for work next week. What a nasty man."

"Oh •ear, look at that woman over there, you •on't wear a bikini like that!"

"Shoul• I grab some chips later?"

"Better not, I shoul• lose some weight."

"But a little pack of chips shoul♦ be okay..."

"I just won't have them with mayonnaise."

"Can't they forbi♦ these ♦ogs over here?"

While the child is enjoying his or her afternoon, our joy gets overshadowed by all kinds of thoughts, anxieties, judgments, irritations, guilt, and our need for control. Life is more fun when the Muppets shut up, which happens in the Alpha and Theta state.

Relax, And Creation Happens Automatically

Remembering that the factory has some gifts to give us, let's connect the 60 bits to the 11,200,000 bits to see how we can benefit from their cooperation. Apart from being a storyteller, our 60 bits have another important function. It is as a coordinator. To further explain this phenomenon, neurobiologist Bernard Baars has developed a metaphor of the mind as a theatre. Now, let's combine this with professor Ap Dijksterhuis's factory and reporter metaphor. Imagine a huge theatre with 200,000 people sitting in the audience and a single reporter with a microphone standing in front of them on stage. If one were to look out into the audience, one could see clearly that everyone is talking, but that it is almost impossible for one person to talk to everyone at the same time from down in the audience. This is where the reporter comes in! The conscious brain can easily talk to the entire factory. Using our metaphor, when the reporter uses his microphone he can reach all 200,000 people at the same time with effortless ease. And even though the reporter cannot control the crowd of 200,000, they can definitely hear him. This has enormous consequences: The unconscious mind has something to consider and work on.

Let's use another example to better appreciate the relationship between our two minds. Say you walk into your garage, get in your car, and realize you left your sunglasses in the house. At this moment, your unconscious brain forgot to grab the sunglasses on the way to the car. Because the sun is shining brightly outside, a group of audience members start to scream at the reporter that your sunglasses are missing. It's at this point that your awareness pops up and you have a thought: "I need to go get my sunglasses from the house," and the rest of your brain falls in line to make this happen. In this way, the unconscious brain uses the reporter to function in a faster and more effective way.

Let's now turn our attention to choices. People love having choices but hate making choices. This is because our brain is wired to be more afraid of losing something than the pleasure of gaining something. As we are afraid of making the wrong choice, having many choices can create a lot of fear, stress, tension, and doubt. If you understand how the 60 bits and the 11.2 million bits work together, it can make choosing effortless.

Every choice you have ever made was created in the factory and you became aware of it after the fact. The unconscious brain is extremely intelligent and incredibly fast. One of its jobs is to assess situations by taking in as many factors as it can when making choices. For example, when buying a car, your unconscious brain is factoring all types of information automatically before you decide to buy or not. It considers the dealership and how clean it is, the trustworthiness of the salesperson, how he is dressed and the way he speaks, how you feel about the color and shape of the car, your previous associations with the particular design or brand, how your reputation will be affected if you buy this particular car, and so on. The unconscious mind is doing an enormous amount of work, effortlessly. Just think about what your life would be like if you had to individually consider all of those factors. Think about the amount of time it would take to list out all of the important factors that need to be considered. Relax! The factory is doing its job beautifully!

What if we told you that neuroscientists have discovered that they can tell what choice you would make even before you have made it? You may think this is a little spooky or even that the scientist is a gifted mind reader. But, that's not the case.

The Illusion Of Free Will

Recently, the world of science has made one of the most important discoveries to date concerning the human brain. Consider this experiment: A scientist places a box with two simple buttons on top of it in front of a person. As part of the experiment, the scientist attaches electrodes to the person's head to measure his brain activity. The person is then asked to choose one of the two buttons to push. No instructions or suggestions are made to the subject. He has full autonomy over which button to push...apparently. When one thinks of autonomy he thinks that the person makes a conscious choice of which button he will choose. And, what would it say if the scientist was able to see brain activity in the unconscious mind that reveals exactly which button would be pushed up to about 200 to 500 milliseconds before the subjects were aware that they had come to a decision? That we don't make conscious choices! All of our choices are made before we are actually aware of them. Really! Is it possible that all of this time we have never really made a rational, objective choice through a top-down, reporter-to-factory process? Yes!

Conscious And Unconscious Choices

Now let's have some fun with this new discovery. Every day you make thousands upon thousands of choices. Most of them are made automatically and unconsciously. Each morning when your alarm goes off you don't consciously think, "Which hand should I use to turn the alarm off?" You just automatically turn off the alarm with the same hand you always do. Then a seeming conscious choice occurs: "Should I push the snooze button just one time or go ahead and get up?" All sorts of thoughts start to pop up. "I need to get up or I'll be late for work." Or, "I'll just take a shorter shower this morning." Or, "I'll exercise in the afternoon instead of this morning."

Once you finally get out of bed, your commute to work also provides a good example. When you are driving your car, almost everything is done unconsciously. Have you ever driven somewhere for 30 minutes and had almost no recollection of how you got there? The car was driven without you being aware of almost any action it took to drive it. You were accelerating, stepping on the brake, passing other cars, and driving accurately around roundabouts. This all happened at the same time you were thinking about your upcoming vacation to Hawaii. So, in actuality, your conscious brain was in Hawaii while your unconscious brain was driving the car for you. Pretty cool, huh? This happens especially on routes that you have driven hundreds of times. But this would not be the case if you found yourself in a foreign country with narrow streets and cars zipping around unpredictably. Your awareness would be fully active. And you'd be using a lot more energy than you would be driving to work each day.

Clearly, many of the things we do and choices we make happen unconsciously. Only a small percentage of our decisions on a daily basis happen consciously. For instance, if you want to lease an apartment, this is not something you do without being aware of it. You might unconsciously choose an apartment with a design that is comforting to you because it resembles the layout of a childhood home but most likely you would not suddenly become aware of the fact that you just leased an apartment. These things you chose consciously, though underlying motivations are housed in the unconscious.

Making Choices Effortlessly

The brain uses our consciousness as a coordinator. So when you have a decision to make, the best thing you can do is to use your 60 bits as a coordinator. If you want to lease an apartment, first scan everything with your awareness. Consider the location, the layout of the apartment, the amenities at the complex, the amount of the rent payment. After this, your unconscious brain will start to process all of the details that might not have shown up in your conscious awareness. The best plan from here would be to simply go get a good night's rest and watch how the answer is given to you the next day. The unconscious brain gives you the answer by making you FEEL what you have to do. It's your intuition or your gut feeling! This is how you chose intuitively while maintaining your awareness.

And this leads us nicely to the true source of our decisions: our feelings. We make hundred percent of our choices based on our feelings. This is because all of our decisions come from our limbic system, where thoughts have no access. Although the brain uses our consciousness to analyze and to overlook the complexity of situations, the final decision comes from beyond the brain. Both of the authors of this book have worked with numerous leaders of companies and had discussions around decision-making processes they employ. And, although some say that they had some type of structure they followed to make important choices, the vast majority relied on something totally different. They always said something like, "I just felt like this or that was the right decision." Or, "I felt it in my gut that this was the right choice!" This might sound strange to a rational leader who believes that he makes conscious decisions all of the time, but from a neuroscientific perspective, it is wise to employ all of your processing power. Most people think that the most powerful way to make a choice is to take all of the information and let the conscious mind go over the details again and again. But this almost always leads to confusion, frustration, and indecision. A more powerful approach is to let the 11,200,000 bits go to work by consciously scanning the situation and then relaxing and letting the unconscious brain do the work. Get yourself in a peaceful state. Take a walk in the park. Sleep on it. It is during these times that the amazing computer in your head will effortlessly come up with the decision.

The Red Pill And The Blue Pill

You might think: "Wait a minute, first you tell me that I have no free will and then you tell me that when I have to choose, it's best to first analyze with my 60 bits and then let the factory make the decision." It does seem contradictory. This is because it is a paradox.

Have you seen the movie *The Matrix*? In this movie, the main character Neo gets to choose between a red pill and a blue pill. If he takes the blue pill, everything will stay the same as it is. When he picks the red pill, they will take him down the rabbit hole toward true understanding. Of course, he picks the red pill. Otherwise, the movie would've been quite boring. We are going to do the same here. We are going to take the red pill.

The blue pill reality is the reality that you have lived in your whole life. You have perceived yourself as being a person, as an I, and it is your experience that you are the one making choices and deciding what you think and feel. This is fine as far as it goes. However, this blue pill reality has a side effect. It creates clouds - all the worrisome thoughts, the frustration, fear, stress, and mental suffering.

In this book, we took the red pill and we could see through the illusion of the "I" and through all the clouds that only exist inside your mind. The saying, "Brahman is real, Maya is real," comes to mind, which points to the idea that the ultimate reality is real and that the illusion is real. Both the blue pill reality and the red pill reality are taking place at the same time. And this is the most important thing to understand and also the most difficult thing to comprehend: You live your life as if you are an "I" and as if you are in control, while at the same everything is simply happening. You can learn to choose more effortlessly and let creativity flow from a calm, focused mind. While you experience that it's you steering the ship, you are simply responding to life as it's happening, and how it will happen regardless of your response. That's the magic trick from the "I" - creating brain.

So you will still live your life as if you have control. It's useful! At this moment, it is my experience that "I" am in control and writing this book. With the insights explored in this book, I know that the words I type are the result of innumerable unconscious processes and influences, even as my conscious mind is reporting that they are MY words and decisions. This message is just one of the tools my brain uses to function. If I were to see this tool as a reflection of ultimate reality and grasp onto my idea of my "self", the clouds would begin to appear. While writing a sentence I might think: "Is this sentence really good enough? What if people think I am crazy? What if people criticize me? This book really needs to be successful or I am a huge failure." From here, the fear clouds gather and darken. Anxiety follows and suddenly I'm deep in writer's block and I reach for a beer and a candy bar to feel relief.

This fear and striving can end. A calm mind arises when one sees through the illusion of the I and we stop identifying ourselves with our thoughts, feelings, and actions in such a serious way.

Snakes And Ropes

Say you walked out of your front door and you see something way down the sidewalk that looks like a poisonous snake. You look around and see you son playing about 20 feet away from it. All types of fear and worry arise. You have terrible thoughts about your son getting bitten and having to be rushed to the hospital. You even imagine how much it will cost and that it may take all of your money to have him treated. You also worry about all of the other snakes that may be in the bushes around the house. To protect your son you start to walk down the sidewalk to kill the snake. As you get closer you realize something: It's not a snake, it's just a rope! Instantly all your thoughts change. You relax and laugh at yourself in your relief. Every fearful thought you had is gone. You see reality. You see the truth. And in seeing this truth everything changes instantly.

When you see the rope you just laugh. That is the power. Once you truly understand that it is simply a rope you can never see it as a snake again. The illusion has been exposed. This is exactly the same thing that happens when one fully understands the true nature of the self. An entirely new, relaxed perspective can arise.

Our True Nature

We already looked at thoughts and can see that they are like clouds passing by. Right now you are looking at this text. Are you this text? No, you are that which is looking at the text. Imagine that a thought pops up. Are you that thought? No, you are that which is looking at the thought. But what is "that"? The most accurate answer is consciousness, because you are conscious of the thought. Consciousness is always there and the thought comes and goes within this consciousness.

Let's say that consciousness is our true nature. This consciousness is only a witness of what comes and goes. If you fall down on the couch with exhaustion, this is being witnessed effortlessly. There is the effortless awareness of feeling exhausted. Exhaustion is simply another object appearing in consciousness. And after a good night's sleep, you notice you feel rested. Feeling rested is also witnessed effortlessly. So if you understand that you are the awareness in which thoughts and feelings come and go – not the thoughts and feelings themselves – there is no resistance to the things passing through consciousness. They simply come and go. Once you identify with a thought or feeling, the drama starts and the clouds pop up.

But what is consciousness? How does it arise, and what is made of? This remains the greatest mystery in neuroscience and philosophy. We simply don't know.

Summary

Life is simple, not easy. We are constantly being challenged by all of life's movements. But it is simple because it simply goes as it goes. Even if there are things you can change, there is no need to worry. Creativity and solutions come from a calm mind, not a worried mind. So relax! Imagine the amount of energy people put in worrying thoughts, frustration, stress, tension, and fear. If you get rid of the clouds, how much extra energy would you have left?

So what does an enlightened leader do with all that energy? They certainly don't spend it going back to the same tiresome grind. They use what they know, effortlessly. As a newly awake leader, it's important first to see through your own clouds. You can only lead people up to the point where you are. How can you liberate people if you are still in a mental prison yourself? Once you are free, you can lead people by helping them understand their clouds and how to see through them. Through doing this you can take away the mental sludge, enabling people to escape burnout and experience more flow.

We want to thank you for reading this book and following us through realizations that can be as uncomfortable as they are liberating. We kept the sentences short and the words simplistic to ease you into your new, effortless way of being. Also, the lady editing this book was quite expensive, so we wanted to keep it as brief as possible. Now that you're done with all of this work, get back to relaxing. We wish you a cloudless mind!

Scott & Paul

Made in the USA
Coppell, TX
09 February 2024

28792181R00066